ROYAL BOROUGH OF GREENWICH

Follow us on twitter @greenwichlibs

Eltham Library
Tel: 020 8921 3452

Please return by the last date shown

6/15

1 1 FEB 2017

2 3 OCT 2017

- 6 NOV 2017

NEW CASE
Jan 2016

GREE

D1100440

3 80

Also by John Kinsella in Picador

Shades of the Sublime & Beautiful

John Kinsella

Armour

PICADOR

First published 2011 by Picador
an imprint of Pan Macmillan, a division of Macmillan Publishers Limited
Pan Macmillan, 20 New Wharf Road, London N1 9RR
Basingstoke and Oxford
Associated companies throughout the world
www.panmacmillan.com

ISBN 978-0-330-51184-1

9 8 7 6 5 4 3 2 1

A CIP catalogue record for this book is available from
the British Library.

Printed and bound by CPI Group (UK) Ltd, Croydon, CR0 4YY

Visit **www.picador.com** to read more about all our books
and to buy them. You will also find features, author interviews and
news of any author events, and you can sign up for e-newsletters
so that you're always first to hear about our new releases.

for Tracy
and to the memory of
Peter Porter,
friend and mentor

Contents

Armour

Burning Eyes

Burning eyes that peer out of a dry crop at night,
shape the seasons and our response —
twin sparks that light the driest stalks
fail to flame, won't combust where you pass.

I see them each night driving home, lit up
by headlights — fox, cat, a rare marsupial
frozen between rows, magnetised by the car's approach.
So frequent over the last fortnight that a pall

of doubt has gripped me: an afterimage I carry
from that first encounter, reigniting in time,
same point every night. I can't bring myself to vary
the plan, to alter the variables; the scheme

of sight, of shine and glint, has trapped
us both. The dry is drying out towards harvest.
Not a vestige of moisture in the stalks — either way,
burning eyes will pass out, lack fuel to conflagrate.

Something must break. I will go away before night
comes to pass as day, or day eats far into night
with burning eyes that peer out of a dry crop.
It's the eclipse of content where compulsion stops.

Owl

Massive owl in redgum surprised
in heavy moonlight by my passing:
a *barn* or *boobook*, quite different
though even a grey-white glow
could not illuminate identity.

So I went back to the place today;
a thin dead branch, not much more than a twig,
that took your eerie weight, phantom bird.
And below, an answer. A component
of the algorithm: a freshly dug mousehole.

A vengeful or indifferent or hungry bird
perched in calculation? Whatever the answer,
I went again tonight to see if your hunting
took you there: opportunistic or logical.
And clouds sweeping over the harsh moon,

what weight their stains would bear.
But you were not there; and why should you be?
It's spring and the mice are opening gateways
everywhere: a vast burrowing and surfacing,
the small weight of their bodies adding up.

Holus-Bolus

The whole bolus of the pocket moon
in the quadrant where I tune
paths through high grass, fire risk,
set alight by friction — boot-frisk.

Need no infra-red, no Night Sight,
just as termites thread de-light,
owls consume mice, sacks of bone,
draw the open ground, mowed zone.

That harvest man, that mower man,
odour of cut and petrochemical tan,
to swoop across the map's day-night
spread, shadows unravelling light.

Mistletoe hang-dog meteorite,
burn up with blue butterflies bright
as all get up, or snakes and blue-
tongues out and about, so too

flyers too quick to identify. Risible.
Goose-egg nest of oats, stressed oval
mowed over without breaking,
not a crack though black veins aching

against the china-white.

The Sleep of Blowflies

The shady side of the house
is covered in blowflies.
It is stinking hot and stormy
and they've stopped moving.

They *might* be asleep.
Or is blowfly sleep a *torpor*?
The house is their corpse
in which eggs won't set,

maggots can't take. No
forensic kit gives clues. The stimuli
of heat and light disrupt
circadian manifests, the sense

of day and night. Memory?
Mushroom body writes
short-sleep lines, struggles
to calibrate sleep regulation

machinery. Opening
a door or window, blowflies
erupt to settle near
places of departure:

too quick for sleep? Resting,
waiting, malingering,
or an attempt to rescue
sleep lost in forensic

etymology, battling
to stay wide awake
in the dark, the swarm
    of isolation.

Aberration

Set in the ranges, the colours switch,
paddocks metallic, wire fences
twitch like vines, saturate and rich
with ultra-Big Bang tints, lenses

highlight semi-articulate crops,
shades off the chart. The kestrel
drops from its post: pulls out the stops,
traverse, rewire, vegetal

rearrangement of the familiar:
a screen to hold out clouds of gnats
so small they'll stress the calibre,
darken streams of sunshine, stats

nightmare. A rodent struck
and lifted up. Green growth silver,
honest to God, and lines that suck
you in: grain birds too fat, odour

of canola, whitewash gleam
of smoothed bark, panorama's
hindsight. See little lambs
steam — take stock O shiny future.

Habitat

False elegies turned on a lathe
enslave the grave clarity of the glorious day
you enlist as scenario, walking brusquely
in lucid morning air. It's not that way
for everyone, but why let that deter you?

Sometimes you stare straight through: ghosting
reliable narrators, making a meal of distance. Visitors,
what the hell would they know! Anyone
who writes locality and convinces
they know better, consigns rare species

to authorial silence. But that's okay,
I say so myself, slipping over in mud
and cutting my arms, face, on scrub. I grow
into the parrots with green tails and yellow hearts
you shoot when they fill your sights. That's

religious: to legislate a pattern. Trees
too wide where water runs, gone, quick as the sun.
Here, a minuscule patch you sing out from.

Gullet

The ground, a gullet, swallows the rain
quick-fire, quick-smart; thirsty as a blank calendar —
never ticked off, days running into each other.
The ground drinks as if it can hold its liquor, drain

gigalitre on gigalitre, a gutful. The cup
runneth over, God knows where, the streams,
creeks, and rivers stay bone-dry: rain poured into seams
of sand, rock, clay; poured through lips

of granite, bristles of the long-gone. Dead sheep
don't drink much, though carcasses
swell, fleeces coagulate: what passes
as comi-tragic when a dry runs deep.

Water resounds like stock epithets, strains
at our neglected gutters — tomorrow
score-marks of run-off, potholes dusty hollows:
the ground, a gullet, swallows the rain.

Sitting in the Car, a Hair's-breadth Away

An easterly shakes the row of salmon gums
deep implanted alongside pocked macadam
of small town with a railway cognomen.
Where you park in shade, meagre at midday,
branches arch out from tumescent cores;
honestly, you'll hear a crack
as premonition, or howl of the kid buried
in the bush cemetery half-an-hour
down the road, buried last century,
crushed by limb-fall, the weight
of top-heavy phantoms, torn
bodies in the dusty terrarium,
where dryness concentrates survival.

The crack comes slight as a door
opening, crack of rifle you hear before
you are down, out for the count,
half-hearing, half-knowing. That's
what happened: we parked the car
in meagre shade; a flaw, a fracture,
a ripping; before I could move the car
it was down behind us, thick as my torso
where it tore from core, no stem cells
innocent enough to knit it back,
to bridge before and after,
test the karma of whatever we value,
mark with its bleakest sobriquet.

Write-off

Night drives home are always fraught
and an eye has to be kept out for kangaroos
and even emus, sometimes foxes and often rabbits
plus owls and tawny frogmouths that swoop
across the parabola of headlights. For a lifetime
I've avoided striking anything large on this road,
though the car grille has choked on insects, has glutted
with plague-season locusts. Picking wrecked bodies
from filaments of radiator, even mangled into one body
with many more legs than genetically encoded, you realise
how large each death will always be. But it seems easier
to forget about than a medium-sized death when windscreen
catches tawny frogmouth and deflects into pitch-black sheets
hung between trees that bleed a phosphorescent orange,
mimesis of the car's disturbing aura, sentinels to body-
counts not added up when cars pass in morning light,
maybe night's carcasses already lifted by foxes
and carted off to veiled dens. This calibrating
of death obsesses you driving home late, keeping
owl-eyes sharp; is shattered when a grey kangaroo
bounds straight out at high speed from the forest;
you swerve to put the balance right and it's there again,
in front of you, a temporal anomaly that slows
world down to words — 'Brace! We're going to hit!' —
followed by impact, radiator meeting fan, fragmenting
into manifold and grinding out valves, cylinders —
flip of carcass past windscreen, over curve of roof,

into the aftermath of passing, wake of darkness, a sickly
tail-lit epilogue of care and obsession. What *are* prayers
really worth to the damaged, to the dead? Prayer is only
about the living, out there, out here, where death is the *only*
conversation. And to glide, brakeless, steering gone,
into an amorphous aloneness, an accident that could go
from bad to worse. To halt without order, without hope,
the car a write-off for what it's worth. And then out
of silence, shots fired in the forest, roos driven out
to escape hunters. Spotlights and dogs that chase
glimmers of eye-light in darkest dark. I know *that* dark —
it's *different*, and fear gives it no special name. I ask
my daughter to lie low in the back of the wreck —
young women can't be seen where there's no escape —
and I try to flag down a passing car. None stops,
intermittent as they are, but I am grateful the hunters
haven't emerged from the forest to check things out. A guy
with dreadlocks pulls up in a truck and relays a message
for help. In dark silence I wait with my daughter — we wait
and listen for roos' heartbeats, for the echo of the dead roo's
heart against shots fired in the dark. I tell her that my childhood
was loud with the pounding of roo hearts, that harm
doesn't mean harm will follow, and that belief works
faster than prayer. Help arrives. We push the wreck
off into a ditch as hunters emerge alert to a frisson
of life in death, mingling of metal and flesh. Spotlights
shine down on the wreck, on rescuers, on us. They rev engines

in triumph, ignoring roo hearts — small, medium-
sized, and large — beating rapidly about us, about them;
louder and brighter than engines, than spotlights.

The Inversion of Simonides' Line about the Sun

Head down on the desk,
he hides tears that force
their way out, warping the ink
of words he can't read.
Isoglosses: smudges of dialect,
script across areas of page,
title deeds to land his grandfather
collated: blocks of mallee,
caprock, breakaways,
map the farm: vast cleared spaces,
fencelines, patches of scrub,
irrepressible cairns of rock
picked when paddock-making,
maintaining: each year upturning
more relic-like granite,
more *history*. His reality.
The teacher approaches
and he chokes on his sobbing.
The family have sent him out,
away from sheep-trails
and furrows, dry winds
and drought: a boarder, home
only on holidays, socialising
with kids his own age,
to confront a language
he neither reads nor writes.

It's your language, they say . . .
it explains who you are,
where you come from.
Why wheat grows
in the light of day . . .
Do you feel ill? teacher
asks quietly. Yes. The sun
is never alone in the sky.

Words of Power

His mother rang
through to school:
'He's on the tractor,
early rains mean
we need all hands
on the farm.' That
was that. His mother
found an old book
in the Salvation Army shop:
Wilfred Funk's
Six Weeks to Words of Power.
'Learn that in two weeks,'
she said, 'and you'll be steps
ahead of those stuck
in the classroom. These New Age
girls who neglect you
will take notice — an inheritance
and brains.' Hunched
over his lunch, out in the paddocks,
he did just that: he gormandised,
abjured his schooling, lacerated
a fox he saw out in the daylight,
taking the Winchester semi-auto
he kept in the tractor
and vilified that vermin's mountebank,
termagant carcass. It was female.
The ravaging rhythm of the tractor

accentuated and burgeoned
his power, his rattling bones
absorbed vocabulary
as if it was natural, passionate,
rodomontade. He would return
to school irascible, acrid and inimical,
excoriate the harridans, satiate
his hurt inner-man with panegyrics
to his voracity, contribution
to the well-being of the nation,
when the crops were in. He would
relocate the teacher's pets, he would define
their turpitudes, opprobriums, and calumnies.
Persistently circumnavigating the paddock,
he traduced the numbness
of repetition; even when bogged down
in heavy ground, plough discs
choked with clay, he remained
stoic in low gear, saw bathos
in crows investigating
the turgid furrows he left
in his wake. I am pertinacious, he laughed,
and it rocks. I am the future
of farming. When I take over
we'll have GPS, we'll knock
nostalgia on the head, like
a litter of kittens,

and I will be implacable
before the girls
who go down to the city
to study, so keen to get away
from the rough and the ready.
Éclat.

Yellow

Tim has been filed
in Yellow Faction
at school. He is frustrated
and angry: he wants to be in
Red Faction, especially for the Cross Country,
which even five-year-olds train for in the Bush.
Character building. Robust. Preparatory.
I take him out to the garden
where I have piled the spent broad-bean stalks,
grey ropes of pea vines,
dead clumps of wild oats,
for a quick burning-off. We are
making ash for the next generation,
I tell him. The fire whips about in the cold
late autumn easterly. It should cut apart
the flames but incites them. Tim,
analytical as always, notes the colour of flame
and distance of colour from the fuel. The orange
and yellow flames furthest away, linger longer,
waver. I say: see, yellow is fast,
and yellow is the colour of the sun,
it is the body of the flames, orange
is the colour of the sun, it is the body
of flames. But Tim is also suspicious
of orange. When he hears a slow ballad
sung in French by, say, Piaf, he says: I don't
like it, it makes me see orange in my head.

He and I, from a distance, consider
the waverings of orange and yellow. He
interrupts the burn-down — smoke making day
night, and wisps of ash fluttering about
like something good — and says: fire
is red too and red is a great colour,
and the flames closer to what's burning
are almost blue. Blue is the fastest colour.
Inside the sun is the blue of our souls.
All other colours are fed by blue
and it makes us fast.
                    A few days ago,
during a sun shower, Tim said that rain drops
don't let some colours of the spectrum
through. Or even let them exist, like indigo,
which *must* be in the fire too.

Dog-Shape Elegy

for Shep

In the dark you baulk, or as
        lightning's leaders
find their mosaic of strike,
        sense which way
to step without tripping over
Shep stretched out, all senses alert,

in his dog-tired sleep-lite phase,
        tiles cooler than air,
a spreadsheet occupation
        of the facts:
our presence he guards:
warning system, gain accolades.

But his shape is absent,
        and you don't trip,
or hear the sigh of disturbance,
        of acknowledgement,
you don't need to settle your
own shape back into place,

shape electrically disturbed,
          hair on end
like his fur standing, touch
          that will come
though it falls away. As outdoors,
his patrolling the boundaries

we put in place to affirm
          our presence,
an occupation of surface
          and depth up
and down though we're not sure
how far either way: how high he can leap

for a ball, dig to bury his secrets.
          This loss
as mechanical as waking,
          as eating
breakfast or lunch or dinner.
Washing and grooming.

That territory might shape
          to fencelines,
a marking as precise as GPS,
          those fences down,
the exact outline is walked,
and confines maintained.

Now roos cross over,
        and foxes,
even rabbits have begun
        diggings:
his presence was their exclusion,
but he let them be at the edges,

he let them be where shape changed
and the howl of a neighbouring dog
        was the only
information he could rely on.

Reverse Anthropomorphism

These birds — western flyeaters — are sizing
me up, making me within their own image,
moi-même, at least for the purpose of hunting.
Through glass, I watch them target their prey,
insects in the temporal zone of the verandah:

one flyeater darts out to seize an insect flyer,
then returns to watch his companion do the same.
The whole time they both keep an eye on me. *Moi-même.*
I connect with them in no way. No displacement
to fill the page: no female pushing a pram

full of letters, 'protecting the male'. Empirically,
they are male *and* female. It seems they perform
the *same* tactics, the same roles when hunting. Role-play?
Who am I to say? Some *would* say it's a matter
of knowing what to look for. *Moi-même.*

This is not a rare experience, it happens most days.
We have grown familiar. Don't mistake my indifference
for their indifference, or their relaxation
for a reflection of mine. We do not share.
Though I am touched that they are near.

And they manage to get done what they
need to get done. It's rich pickings
near where I sit, separated by the glass window,
insects making their own conversations,
losing lives. *Moi-même*. Role-play.

Cutworms

Night's redecorators test thin stems
of the newly risen, sample with gnashers
that'll take down a forest,
just above the surface.

What is sweetest, a triumphing
before the succulence thickens,
hardens to trunks, holds forth bloom
and seed and stands up to the sun

even when green has faded, vascular
urge is lost. Sharp as necessary,
maybe even sharper, you can't compare
to human tools of cutting,

slashing. Though incisors
mix media, to fell that tall timber,
for here flees a grey pudginess
as bogong moth, flies

out of its skin, its cage, its crib,
so sleepy in summer wings,
so willing to fly far and wide,
gathered together.

Distended Triolet

I go out and search, as I've searched many times over;
trace an encephalograph in the upturned stump's biomass;
lichen on root-stock tests photosynthesis, its non-fungal partner.
I go out and search, as I've searched many times over;
black-faced cuckoo-shrike, hunting, perched among the citrus
tilting over — garden bush amalgamation; exculpation;
I go out and search, as I've searched many times over;
trace an encephalograph in the upturned stump's biomass.

Where the Almond Tree

Where the almond tree died, so died the wattle.
That parabola can take no life for long. If borers
      are below the surface,
they will move on. They have killed the already dead.
When the last leaves fell they flagged independence:
      thin acacia leaf became the hearted leaf
of the almond: it all added up in going. Parrots
      still poke about looking for almond kernels,
but they don't stay long. They alter the angle
of their tails and get out of there. Sometimes
      I let them fly through my head —
a perversion, but not sexual. They get a lift
out of it and I clear the static. Hooking up over
      India, Afghanistan, and on to Europe,
the jumbo jet sticks carefully to its flight path.
      War is about flight paths
as well as fuel. I watch the flight map
for those hours it takes, with mixed feelings,
      as if I have that right,
as if I am tracking testimonies. It bothers me
the almond tree died so intensely
      it lost all moisture. And the wattle
died just as entirely. There's not a lot of water
      to go round, but I shed
what I can in the parabola that can take life
      no longer. Parrot feathers
are flags. They fold up at rest. Fly at half-mast.

Easterlies

for Peter Sculthorpe

1.

We fear the brouhaha of mood
and tones of inaction, to decamp,
to extract myths from country
and myths hard let go from reading

a vicarious sense of being,
of having come from wherever
myths implant. Dust stings.
We are blinded by howlers.

The long seeding grasses
suddenly dry. Shaken empty.
From whips to whispers. Exhausted.
Freshwater snakes huddling,

desiccated as the riverbed.
Toads, deep buried, vulnerable
to evaporation. Scattering
of salt deposits.

        To call upwind
is to singe lips and perish,
no matter how loving
your speech:

        we must hope,
fire-risk, a cold lunch
spread on the table.
Grit in our mouths. Fire.

2.

Time passed makes a tinker's cuss,
pressure on the solar plexus,
today's easterly is a cut above,
cut from a differing cloth:

desert blankets
where cold is dry.
April now, far away
from first-draft wildfires,

a smothered time of burning-off,
cold morning blasts
hacking with smoke
turned to ash and dirt.

What effect can light have?
Monet's times of day. Light
influences light itself, howling
without the sun, self-made.

Glitter and fallout.
As others add layers
to keep it out, I stay
in my t-shirt

braced and withered,
gleaning sensation
as my frame shakes,
ribs against the sun,

selfishly gathering
the harsh and the sharp,
windward — numb —
a windsock in the adjacent

paddock braced red,
shout narrowing to where
the wind is going,
going, gone.

I remember the levanter
from when I was young,
on an island of the Mediterranean,
alone, weather rushing in.

3.

All easterlies are cold now,
their blaze extinguished,
and imperceptibly
stretched out

into a monthly
cycle: the cold
catching you,
breathless,

the garden bonfire
tense with conflict.
It's easy to think seasons —
ironic schemes of things —

endnotes
of an elegiac
pastoral.

Idyllatry

1. *Laetiporus portentosus*

It has weathered the storms, though its white
punk posture has injected rot into the heart
of the eucalypt, and its pore surface,
green sheen of a mirror more luminous
than glass, is breached by numerous
invertebrates, larvae that will interphase
with our sense of space, the air
we breathe, prayer-trace and outdoor
embrace of change and surprise:
such brackets we hinge on, use
to prise apart our rituals, distract from grief;
halo we might walk beneath,
and so the first people here carried fire
in its smouldering tinder.

2. *The View from Here and Now*

The river froths as it passes the pagoda —
a treated-pine viewing tower — a turgid glow
of rapid water that deludes us into thinking
the river has compunction, that gnats

enjoy being eaten in their clouds
along the banks, in niches where froth accretes
and run-off steadies, where local currents
tap the biorhythms of invertebrates —

but the point is in *pagoda*, a structure of aesthetics
and utility, or rather, a one-leaf stupa
that's technically not a pagoda: more likely
an elevated gazebo, perched on trunk legs,

daring the river to flood upstream
down. The rush of water drowns
out tiny birds, though the croak of a blowsy
heron untangles the gentle rapids.

The crux is recurrence at times of tension,
when distress is offset by the boardwalk
and this 'viewing platform' — locals
prefer the understated and rarely visit.

Low-key and focal, anomaly of here
and now, oddity of permanent pool
when once they were standard, a facsimile
of water, tourist stopover, fate

of floodplain. And what breaks
the bursts of wattlebloom, takes
paperbarks for granted, insert
of amenities, these local assets.

3. An Idea of Disorder

The observations are no longer startling,
fresh, or evocative. Familiarity can't even
breed the contempt to drive you out
of the picture. The most exquisite,
fragile birds, don't stimulate

the synaesthesia effusion
that compels you to wake,
look out into the scrub, and pray
for arrivals. Senses have compacted
or been put on hold. Metaphor

has been abandoned, or rather,
the anatomy remains intact as gesture,
and the flesh stripped away: sheep
dumped on the edge of the reserve
where the burning-off risk is taken

to its limits, perverse as title deeds
and 'but up to that line it's my land'
scenarios. Flesh and clumps of wool
detached from the frame. I hear
a gunshot. There is no follow-up.

Pot-shot at a fox, the gun behind the seat
of the ute, parked next to the truck with its bin
loaded with seed-wheat, the air-seeder
of a brother or son out in the swales
of the paddock. In that part

they didn't burn off this year,
seeding into the remains of stubble,
tying the soil together that would otherwise
float away in plumes of dust over summer.
As it is, they're almost dry-seeding,

hoping for the rains. I don't believe
it's about routine. I don't care what our
calendar says, how temperamental
the barometer is, what cock-crow
does to the psyche, dragged out

of bed before dawn has a fix
on the land, making alterity
out of its half-haunted light that not all
of us will see. Anyway, it's all lies.
I've spent half my life living

in the middle of this and don't believe
any of it. I don't believe in growth,
and I don't believe anyone's being fed.
The grain flows out into the world's
granaries and there's a food shortage.

I've whinged over and over about how
we're poisoning country, sucking the land
dry for short-term gain. But what of it?
This is my swan-song. I've nothing
more to add to the litany, the testament.

Maybe I've become like Mallarmé
always was, in his war-tuned 'Petit Air'.
I see the approach of the infantry.
I translate, tucked up close
to the Bushman Stove.

Shortly, I'll head into town.
The further out you live the more
shopping becomes 'for supplies'; that we
might be cut off, and have to rely
on what's stockpiled. Earthquake, storms

that decimate roadside trees
blocking the roads, flash flood
through the valley. All of these
have happened over my life here.
What's more, there's an army camp

less than thirty ks away, so a military
solution is never more than a drill-depth
away from the surface. Two years
ago I wrote to the state premier
suggesting a 'wheatbelt forum'

where indigenous communities
could discuss their issues with white
farming communities: a place of respect,
of working things out. The idea
was enthusiastically met, but like

most things out here, vaporised.
'White farming communities' . . . is this
accurate? Maybe. Here, the idea of whiteness
resonates. At school, our son is learning
Nyungar ways, and we are proud

of his pride in sharing Nyungar culture.
He wants to be Nyungar. We have to tell
him that is wonderful, but he can't be Nyungar.
He can respect, but he can't be. Therein
is the pain of this place, the pain

of myths that are real, stories that are fact.
The Wagyl really is in retreat as the river grows
more and more saline, fresh water holes
grow more and more brackish. We know
where it hides. That's true. It's not

a matter of belief. So, here's what I
see from where I sit: stands of York gum
with track-marks set by termites, jam tree
weighed down by mistletoe, a black-
shouldered kite circling above the dead

York gum, just skin and bones, we mark
the intensity of storms by — it loses bones
proportional to the blast — willy-wagtails
working the in-between spaces for insects.
The air, inside and out, reverberates

with the actions of farm machinery.
I feel no guilt not being out there, helping.
I cherish the action of the flora and fauna,
but have nothing to observe that might
traumatise those around me into

preserving the habitat. Overhead,
climbing, jet aircraft make their way east.
There's a navigation marker on the hill
behind us. A place of rare species of orchids.
Of the oldest stories. I can't bear to look

back at it, having nothing to add.
But looking up, even though it's a darkish sky,
an early morning fog having lifted
indecisively, can make out the contrails,
reflecting heat back to the myths of creation.

4. Idyllatry

A tractor's roar underscores
heavy-going ground, the kookaburra
makes its claim, ricocheting. Why moribund,
the growth season, a caul of sound?
Nexus of malpractice, horse whisperers
casting spells and hanging horseshoes
on loungeroom walls? Woodsmoke
fills their wells — providence, alpaca wool
starting to spill; we cannot
stand the winter sun's pale affront,
green gestures of the spread, barbed wire's
limped glint, the fencer's iffy scrawl! You
cannot hide the dust within the urn,
its plumes within the fog. Fungi
make the most of our equivocal elation,
but keep to themselves: a tropic underscore
of cellular motion far from the cold;
as we'd impose, as splits the seed with tail
to ground, libidinal stretch towards display;
to spend this meagre soil — for that's its name
when wet, for wet hides dust's derelictions. Worship
in churches goes like the clappers, clustered
against any glister of winter: call down storms, call
down lash of gossip and may the creeks
and river run white water, gasp

on granite rapids, unfurl heads of steam
and wash negligence out to sea. Worship,
eyes to the page, voice to rafters, you'll hear
the kookaburra ricocheting, come lately, but breaking
through the glass-ceilinged egg of their world,
joyous as picking fights or giving birth,
or taking up your inheritance.

Processional Caterpillars
Mistaken for Spitfires

From writhing ball of the intermingled
that don't inflict upon each other, no hair-
line fractures, no collective urticaria,
they peel off tail to head, a procession
of dead giveaways, to ward off
the predator, to cast the illusion
of holism, one-ness, the serpentine.
They know their myths of origin.

And deception. Word of mouth,
their inheritance is narrative, a route
of lines — silk spat out, woven as cable;
daylight manoeuvrings, slower than night
when they break away to feed
on jam tree, to shed hairs and frass,
enthusiastically. Individuated.
But now, in their tunnel-

vision, they are anything
but the keen-sighted caterpillars
that have flight and travel written
so expansively into their muscular
bodies. Those eyes, those tussocks
of body hair rampant as prickly pears
outside abandoned farmhouses.
At first, it was suggested

they were spitfires. We all recall
them from childhood, but not quite like these —
enough similarity to wonder, though? No. They
follow the leader up the embankment,
over a raging ant nest, back down
to gravel to carve their channel
through dust. This takes ages.
A bristling queue where none jumps.

Steady. Steady. They spirit-level
perfectly, threaded from mouth to anus,
anus to mouth, breathing out
of their sides. Migration? Exile?
Surface or interiority?
Halting as the sun intensifies,
breaking formation, reforming
to gradually scale the veranda wall

up into the rafters, to curl
and exchange and weave
a communist utopia . . . or revel
in mutual aid, destiny not as determined
as they tell each other? Who among them
will take the lead when they next break
out — ships of the line? Heave ho, onward,
haul the sheets. We *have* discovered

a name — these are no spitters,
and their fire is irritation, *Ochrogaster*
lunifer, whose inflammations
we respect, and worship the single-mindedness
of their collective. So, deliverance
isn't up to any one of us,
though we are all impelled,
though we all like to feed?

Dip

But a dip is subtle, you're down
and lowland is 'as the case might be',
a benign memory like wading through a creek
in hot weather, trousers rolled up to the knees,

all complexity quelled by the feeling
of smooth stones massaging your feet,
though it's rare for water to flow here, or there,
in summer. Storms as pleasure.

Down to the dip, DIP sign shot through
with holes, rust coronas, like looking inside
out through the puys of the Massif Central,
Auvergne, at this semi-green time of year.

You barely decelerate, and anything
that approaches will slip up onto you.

Hyperbole

Patois of the shredder,
shoddy skinner, demi-
pruner of roadside vegetation.
Poète engagé, ha! I pursue data,
inform my protest,
wrest lyrics from the brutal,
but the name of this rotator,
psychopathic cutter,
is hidden, encoded.

Travelling, I have caught
its progress, high-pitched
whirring, nerve destroyer,
too often — a seasonal
assignation, slasher
moment from which
the ghost-self emerges
tattered as living
and dead flesh mixed.

Truth is, I know
the operators, know
the work they crave: a call,
a few hours, a shire
pay-cheque. Just enough.

Today we flayed the garden.
At smoko we ribbed and jibed,
exaggerated the assets
of celebrities.

Mostly, that cutting whirr.
Mostly, the screeching banshee.
Mostly, the screaming ab-dabs
this machine induces.
Short-tempered
with the kids. I hear
this — it is said among friends.
For their sakes, also,
I protest, *poète engagé*, ha!

Dust Funnel Cloud

The entries to hell that circumvent
      have twisted into one, a conduit
straight to heaven, a vast unplugging,
a feeding the cloud-base, vast paddocks
of dust sucked up and rained down
      as drought. Driving
towards Tammin, fixed on monumental
wheat silos, stark white, we saw it rise out
or *descend* upon scrub, collude
      between with centrifugal
force, neither meteorology nor superstition
      joining a bedraggled patch of wodjil —
worn out and thirsting, leaves powdering —
to top-heavy clouds bulging
      through humidity.
      It whipped back and forth,
rare — if-ever-seen-here — twister,
like a builders' chute swallowing scraps
      of masonry and waste,
shitting it out into a rusted skip;
      but *this* worked in reverse,
long and slender as the throat
of a vacuum cleaner, coiling
      dust like a cord.

We wanted it, pursued it. To come
        close enough, let others know
        what they'd be up against:
the funnel letting go before it could grab us,
before anyone noticed us missing.

Inland Cemetery: Extreme Heat

Heat bends headstones.
Crosses break a shaky surfacing —
wrecked on a brooding hill-line.

Bright wreaths of plastic
and 'new materials' wither.
Oil from eucalyptus leaves
so volatile mourners gasp.

Plots expand beyond splitting,
cracking — until contractions
of evening, not a sound is heard.

Fierce, decorative birds
claw dead souls waiting
to effervesce into darkness,
ride the cool change.

Resurrection Plants at Nookaminnie Rock

They're full-blown in their early spring
rush — pincushions a fakir's bed of nails
so soft to tread on, so easy to make false
comparisons by, and all the baggage *that* carries —
rest-break on a granite slab looking out over
the island sea of scrub shaded with formations
beneath a green lagoon's surface. It's what we
bring to the apogee before the drying-off,
dead crunch beneath our feet as rock-
dragons wake to the heat, and emphatic
belief that the dead will stay dead
and there will be no lift, no rebirth,
wherever you come from, whatever
you believe. Step carefully around these
wreaths hooked into granite sheen, holdalls
for a soil-less ecology, a carpet you know
would say so much more if your boots
were off and skin touched life brought
back, restored, gifted, bristling with death
because death is the most alive district
to inhabit. We could say so much more
        if only we had the time.

Quake

Where the church cracked in the quake
we could open and see the people;
lines are decades old but invoke
those moments of being fearful.

The flooded gums that hold the river
are dying before red roots reach
foundations — prayers deliver
either too little or too much.

The sun pulls the town together —
hint of green, frosty mornings;
church door is locked to outsiders,
cracks follow mortar, bricks, bell rings.

Wreck

The boy who is not yet a man is walking slowly,
    almost trudging across the sludgy ground
        towards the machinery shed
        where his father is welding.

The boy who is not yet a man will become 'a man of few words',
    but now is searching, is scanning all the words
        he knows, and all the ways
        he knows of planting them in sentences.

The boy who is not yet a man realises that his face,
    the expression he will try to hide, will
        nonetheless be like a novel,
        a portrait painting, a police report.

The boy who is not yet a man replays the moment over
    and over in his head, projecting it large
        in his mind's eye so that he might
        understand, better explain how it happened.

The boy who is not yet a man knows the tractor
    will rear up on its hind legs, frothing at the jaws,
        and writhe before dropping dead. He can see
        himself riding it into the ground, defeated.

Hay Cutting

Mandibles that reject their meal,
a compulsive spitting out, 'nary
a drop down the hatch', some might say,
full of whimsy and demi-cultures

as if chomping through mixed metaphors;
but digestion begins in the mouth,
and the snapping of the still-green stalks
impels the breakdown, lifeforce

essentially cut off mid-flow, in its rush
to push seed to completion. The farmer-operator
wants the seed attached to the body,
to bale with stalks full-caches of goodness,

replete with nutrients. The hay mower —
rakes in rows, for rows are easier.
Easier to manage. Easier to consider.
As each day the cut moves towards the centre.

The circumlocutions of the day before —
strips and bands of hay — such are windrows,
such the exposure to the quickest
dry possible. The earlier rows,

drier and lighter — a tonality.
Despite hayfever and hard work,
there's a lifting in moods. But not
for quails and other small birds.

And the snakes have just woken
and are after the mice. The causality
of mice. Gwarders and bobtails
move laterally. Cataclysm and profit.

The roots of the crop live on longer,
and hold the soil together. A raft.
But the machine is at the centre,
and behind it our driver. Hay

is embryonics; hay is cryogenics:
taking the cure it's held for as long
as possible. If the markets collapse
he'll still cut hay, and store
          it for longer.

Work Rural Work

Rural isn't a lifestyle,
it's an equation of work:
a quota filled that leaves
hands gnarled and calloused,
that indoctrinates through blisters
and dust on the lungs. Rural is ploughing
at night and tasting diesel in your sandwiches,
it's dreaming of the Southern Cross and riding the plough
up over the tractor's duals, it's pulling supernovas of caltrop out
in the bleeding sun, when all else around is dead
and tinder-dry, and the caltrop green as a jungle
risen in response to rain a fortnight back,
a storm that brought down the rotten limbs of York gums
you realised could have wiped you out. Rural is hay-
carting for a neighbour when every cent counts
and fatigue is dryness and moisture, a cement of sweat
that is the sea cucumber spitting its guts out
to ward off predators; rural is fencing
which as hell goes is complete in itself: the rips
and tears of flesh secular rosaries or prayer wheels
or candles lit for your youth. Rural is not the visit
or the hike or memories of childhood watching
others work. I know that, and my bloody hands
know that, their own kind of supernovas
burning far off, unrecognised and nameless,
having no time to rest before working,
turning over the mass of the universe.

Beetopic or Beetopia?

Indifferent to imagery and choreography,
the bee colony intense with the sparseness
of pollen — only wattles and some eucalypts
are in blossom. Near the hamlet, in the hollow
of a York gum — fruits of dead core,
living tree eaten out, dead bone within
living bone, all trace of age digested like ritual —
a message from Rumi, master of the whirling
dervishes, implanted like compassion shaped
as 'hive' amidst 'nature', God's exotica,
we are annihilated, forgetting consequences,
disciples threaten, letting the 'wild' be 'wild'
and the farmed be farmed, a cartoon-gimmick
in the age of cinematography: Australian
cinematographers famous for their clarity,
preciseness of imagery exported across
the world stage, elevation of local
to a universal chatter, blasphemy
holy and healthy, desirable.
Within the hive, within the nest,
admire warily, as politics
is proximity cross-pollinating
to make food an essential alibi,
performing to be heard, to gain
right of entry, see in and out
of the dark heart
where the queen works
the crisp cold of a valley winter.

The Decay of Hemispheres: a Defence
of Mathematics

The pocked surface where small boulders
have been lifted — half-submerged, half-bulging — levered out;
    the weight of rock
we compile as something solid, the impression
of volume out of the soft soil:
    capillaries of root
    that clasp around
    the lifted hemisphere,
    wild oat seeds that have fallen
    green into the opening, the mould, a scattering of sand;
the brainwork
of roots exposed to light, sticks
in the mind's eye: what's in our heads: or model their grip
        as total surface area
of hemisphere — lifted, retained
before erosive movement changes shape,
the trigonometric
        observations. The decay of small insects,
their carapaces stuck to our boots, skin: shining.
I favour $3\pi r^2$
a totality of hemi, a pathfinding *breve* or *arch*
that takes its shortened vowel,
            that arches
to join the path
    cleared to mow: even so,
        the mower

is a write-off,
                the blades having struck rock,
glanced off the hemispherical top,
                                lifted the sphere
out and shattered the bearings, shredded
the drive belt: rubber and metal,
                                heat transfer
                and deformation, which intensifies
a memory of metal-making:
adiabatic shear bands,
                                maybe even the metalwork of shearing
equipment: the tension in a handpiece,
the cutting of wool,
                of sheep; and the indentation,
as smooth as roots,
                not a violent stroke
recognisable: soothed. So much silence
through winter,
                inflected in the cut green,
the die-off at this time of year.
                                Distracted,
I wander outside the frame of clearing,
                                of keeping
the grass down
                for coming fire-season: the nocturnal
brush-tail possum
                dead on the side of the road,

and then a few hours later — broad daylight — another
stretched over the bitumen,
                        I am distracted
from the maths of work
by the horror of movement:
                        of seeing:
brush-tail laid out, glinting, hemisphere of head
a grisly spectre of volume, total surface area,
spread,
        carbon content fragmenting
over the carbon-coloured
surface; how long dead? We know
parameters
            having passed by earlier.
Fossil presence of the *just* dead.
            Decay constant?
$dN/dt = -\lambda N$
            I start from this equation.
The symbols
            hook me like a burr,
        a tooth,
                an ogonek or an eth accent.
As I walk back
            through the mowed,
        semi-mowed area:
hemisphere on hemisphere,
                    memory on memory:

old as a lost friend,
          old as the brush-tail possums
so recently dead
                    and glaringly translucent
as the brainwork
of roots opened to sunlight,
                              dash through light
to its dead mate, already
exponential decay
          opens skull's windows
to release
          the radioactive build-up,
the coming up
              through the floor,
night and day:
              it's what we do
        to survive
the saga.

Childhood Phenomenology
of the Opposite Bank

Crossing the river
by hemistiches:
you have only been halfway
across, in a dead-straight line,
each time you hesitated
and swam back. From the diacritical
brevity and precision of the river-beach
at the end of Cranford Avenue,
cosseted by paperbarks,
so familiar to you,
you launch into
the brown water
to swim over
to the other bank,
an epic. You squeeze
through the ghost-touch,
threshold of jellyfish
drifting in their bondamines —
where space between is not space,
but implied stress, and your tendency
to pull left, swimming overarm,
is exaggerated by the abject,
though the bank
remains directly ahead,
unstressed with river-reeds
signalling against your panic.

To reach the black mud
suction of the river's
other lip is murder,
and your loss is fact,
to see the gentle beach
as your sanctuary, sure
that you'll never join
the halves together,
make the line across
the river, stretched below
a patchy sky and the sun low,
tell its story. With evening
the kingfish will run
and slice the river
in two.

Sand Tale

'covering all'
Tracy Ryan

Tracy and I are less than two years apart in age.
We have similar but different experiences of growing up.
We both emerged in the same corner of the world.
I did high school in the country, she did a bit of primary school
in the country. We both spent a lot of time in Perth
when Perth was different. She was from a suburb
bordering the hills, I was from an inner river
suburb that bordered hundreds and hundreds
and hundreds of acres of bush, as well
as a swampy limb of the river
that became a creek. Old Bateman's farm
was down there, and cows got stuck
in the silty riverflats. Tracy spent
most of her time in her suburb,
I spent a lot of my time
out of the city. At the farm,
or maybe north to see my father. Sand
was big in the city but rare on the farm. Red-brown dirt
up there. Not sand that'd pour through your fingers.
Not sand that was black and let water run
through like there was no end to the earth.
Not sand that was yellow as if it had been dyed,
sickly and sweet at once. It would set rock hard.

Being hit by a rock of that could break your skull.
Not white sand that would grow nothing
but looked and felt so clean. Sandpits.
Pleasure. Fetish. Exhuming the lost,
lifted out as easily slipped in and away.
Hungry, but ready to give it up. Brought
in from the beaches: the thin river beaches
in need of topping up. At night, early in the morning,
shovel and sacks, robbing the public,
the behest, the dyadic self.
The flat discs of jellyfish: moon translucent,
never quiet: you see nothing but sand caked on their
eating parts. Or the spotted mottled brown
jellyfish with its bunched-up, thick
tentacles, cloying beads of sand. That's what
comes of endosymbionts, tossed up in their armadas.
Their multiplicity is sandlike and yet
we draw few analogies from it. Like brown jellyfish
in the hourglass. As if humour is everything
in childhood, and we're not serious and bleak
drying on the sand, digging so it will collapse,
so it will give way. The edifices to be knocked down,
eaten by breeze and slight tidal shift of the river.
Though in winter the jetties gulp for breath,
sand in cracks floats out. Sand of the river,
slowly making its way down
to the river mouth. Sand that sets

when you come out of the murky
river, a Swan River whaler sighting,
and all your tension about swimming lessons
sets as a new skin that dries and cracks and even
peels away. That sand too. But there was no
real sand up at the farm. If it poured
it was as dust, up there, in the valley. Clouds
that swarmed and rolled and choked.
The fine film that covered
like a lyrical aftertaste. Gritted your eyes,
but you didn't need to pick the grains out,
finer, it wept away. But where
I went to school in Geraldton — coastal town
where sand plains are farmed against the lack of rain,
where you travel inland to search out the stony country
of the next people, the Yamatji elder telling his mate
that he's crossing over just about now,
on the road to Mount Magnet.

Zoo Visits

He polished his car to a shine, he kept
a 'clean machine' inside and out, but down
from 'up north', the red dirt would stay
in the seams of doors, around the fittings.
A detailing of distance. A truth unto itself.

What to do with us, having travelled
so far — the access-visit conundrum, divorced
bloke's existential crisis. Kids aren't going
to live on feelings alone for an afternoon,
they want entertainment. Time is action.

The zoo excursion undoes its own irony —
the cages more than conceits, more than
allegories of maintenance and child support.
The babies of most species cling to their
mothers, and that's got to hurt. The smell

is so prevalent — we called it 'a stink',
the kind we gave off when badly behaved
and told off: a fear reaction. We were brave
leaning in through iron bars thick as Dad's arms,
knocking at the armour of the rhinoceros,

as wagtails picked insects off. Could it feel
their delicate feet? Its horn, worn down
to a stump, looked anything but mythical.
Rough skin fascinated us — the elephant's,
the hippopotamus rolling in its baby bath.

The fairy penguins launched from their castle
into a moat of fast food, and that was a talking
point. Penguins and coke cans. Magical. Like
pythons in glass boxes or the smoking gorilla.
Time is action. And our dad glanced at his

watch out of anticipation. We didn't get that.
We were too busy making metaphors. The mini
railway wound its way around the heartlands.
Safari. The sound of species lost since then.
Zoological gardens. Family crisis centre.

The polar bear mauled someone who jumped
into its green waters. It leapt off its white ledges
bothered by no melt, ate, and covered its bloody
black nose. It happened before and after Dad
talked of its power. He liked the bears. And the cats.

He wanted us to like them. The big animals.
The big dads. Keep away from the edge,
he said in a way that meant more to us than
an excursion; than entertainment; than time.
Than the car he polished to a red dirt shine.

Sea Shanties

THE SWAY OF A COASTAL PINE TREE

A lipidic white-capped sea, low
coastal heath, tether tableaux
to breeze bending the old pine
towards them, its sway on rebound
bringing it back to lash sunset.

Bright dark matter mixed
to force back to where the breeze
has blown, to fill compulsive
need, sweep to vacate and occupy —
lean to resist, impelled.

Pine is ritual, drawn back
to depths where appearances
are made and blessed, mast-like,
bent against a tidal surge,
branches radiant with drowning.

Confess, to balance or divine
a flow, draw needles against compasses,
steer towards an anchorage,
high up in the rigging, less rigid,
        breeze-dried waves,

arrangements of vastness.

WRECK AT COOGEE BEACH (1905−)

When Mum swam
the belly of the wreck
keelhauled over periwinkles
sand glowed where abattoir blood ran,
secrets of electricity spilled — power plant
perched on rocks overhead.
The deck closer to the sand,
          closer to the sand.
Gulls thick about the bowsprit.

Clinker hull, jackass barque,
carried cables for the overland telegraph;
made us who we are, in part — brothers
of the sand; rush to discover
where waves lap and storms
lash embryos of flotsam — whiting
and garfish at the deeper end,
octopuses gripping a broken stern.
The deck closer to the sand
          closer to the sand.
Gulls thick about the bowsprit.

When the *Omeo* broke its moorings
within the Sound, gale lashed
its aged body — that Mum might swim
her childhood again, write
the wreck as folklore; and we might
swim away or play the sand or lose
all thoughts of inland.
The deck closer to the sand
closer to the sand.
Gulls thick about the bowsprit.

With all these tricks: *watch me! watch me!*
dive into sheltered waters, dive
where sea filled with effluent,
where sharks dizzied in bloody fluid;
let backwashed footprints
push up to reset perfect
sandy pictures, lit by kelp.
The deck closer to the sand
closer to the sand.
Gulls thick about the bowsprit.

What I Saw off Cheynes Beach

Seeing the black eyes of white pointers
some people want to poke them, to take these sea-
giants out with one small finger, 'defensive'
mastery greater than dragging

sperm whales in from the continental
shelf, those old Norwegian chasers
cutting through a whale slipstream,
the passages they know. So, at five
years old I stand on the warped

white sands of the beach, holidaying,
looking out into the bay at the flagged
carcasses of whales, mountains in the blue-black
ocean, disturbed like a split lip spitting
froth and fear, bobbing though so lifeless

I wonder what living is, sand too cold
beneath your feet, too cold in my long pants
and windcheater, the stench of flensing
and boiling down, teeth piled high,
seawater and blood and spermaceti

of the whaling station — reason for the town —
reason for posturing against the French,
an American connection from the beginning
they wished to make, filling the oil-lamps
of readers in cities around the globe.

Seeing the black eyes of white pointers
I wonder if they are one-eyed, orbicular
to the one side, to keep an eye out,
thrusting up on to the dead whales, side-
swiping jaws ripping skin and blubber

and I know then blood comes out of the dead
though it flows differently — I've already
cut myself severely — and the dark ocean
makes a different viscosity, an attracting
and diluting flow that is scent for sharks

to follow in, to rasp atmosphere over great gills
as they emerge like dolphins, but ample and rough
and with a new take on grace: who is to say,
this beautiful flesh-death, death in death,
so energised as they bite the air, our seeing.

All of me, all of Mum, and all of Dad
would fit into one of those white pointers,
giant finned barrels propelling teeth,
but I don't think that at the time,
on the shore, looking out at the blue-black-red

collars of blood, the growing number
of sharks, the glut and the feast and the strange
angles of biting and tearing and looking at me
not so far away but far away from shark mind
so single-mindedly completing its plan,

its awareness, its line of thought: the news
I will tell the following year when I start school,
my grandfather in the spotter plane, the thrill,
the chase, the history of harpoons and the anger
it will make in me and the blood it will fill

me with that's not red but froths with history
and witness and a dull science that quells fear
and vengeance even though my brother
will surf where surfers are taken, are snatched,
all of them saying, 'leave them be,

these great creatures', the driven and logical
giants who know their own company
and the cartilaginous nature of ocean
so solid and flexible and churned up
with all that we call matter, all

that post-Enlightenment posturing
we laugh at and over in our secular
worship, those large blips on the sonar,
those seeing black eyes of white pointers.

THE DEAD

'Amour, peut-être, ou de moi-même haine?'
Paul Valéry

We can't find the graves though we know
they should be here. A holiday park
dilates like a coronary artery,
its interlock fence an expanding ribcage

grafting pine trees and lawned area
and the seaside cemetery. Now the dead
aren't 'just over the fence', they're camping
in the grounds of the holiday park,

bunking down for the night
at twenty dollars a site. The sea
sucks and spits at their berths,
though limestone retainer walls

have been set against the grain-
by-grain reaching-out of bones
for the sea, where relatives lie,
sunken and dissolved;

that once-in-a-generation storm
reaching out, grasping
headstones, shipwreck ink
on a map that lacks names, directions.

I tell our son about Buccaneer,
a game from my father's childhood,
in its blue cloth-covered box
a scrolled map, wooden boats

with paper sails and toothpick masts,
tiny gold bars that tarnished,
pearls that were droplets, diamonds
that trapped the light and kept it,

rum in wooden barrels.
We didn't know the rules.
So many ships wrecked
the length and breadth of this coast,

chronometers and sextants
seeding new reefs, privateers,
colonies of the dead. At the end
of a stormy famine highway

they dropped into the sea,
into cross-currents and weather,
sighting tall trees
and a rocky coastline

a dying language, like theirs.
Strange how uneasy you feel,
graves deleted and slept over,
ribs of the ship snapped off

to grow you, your child.
And holiday-makers
in the park, drinking, laughing,
arguing about the risks of sunburn.

Demand to know where they lie.
Your dead. What placed them
in private hands, at the service
of this 'vibrant' coastline.

Megamouth Shark

'About the Shark, phlegmatical one'
Herman Melville

Should we be grateful they're not claiming
it as art, but as science? Or are they smugly
doubling up — the art of preservation the boon
of research? Megamouth, so rare it wasn't recorded
as science until 1976, day-time deep dweller
off the continental shelf to rise at night to a lesser
depth, to graze screeds of plankton we barely
register? So much for autonomy and agency
in the great body of water. Megamouth, 'rescued'
from death in shallows to depthless formalin, embalmed
within stainless steel tank-of-the-dead, necropolis
aquarium so shiny and technical, with portholes
for us to peer through, its saucer eyes staring out
with a vision we can't configure, though the designer
can. The electric pump to keep preservative circulating
is eternal as power and its grid, as the toxic ocean
pulsing in the harbour. New centrepiece of the maritime
museum, its sails parsing the stiff sea breeze. Comparisons
are fuel for the patronising, and I can't help but think
this tank and its inhabitant are prescient fulfilment
of *Dune*, a pox on emperor houses of curators
and scientists, this Guild Navigator the benign

encapsulation of Edric shrouded in orange gas,
so distorted to outside eyes, plotting the courses of ships
through space without collision, devastation like anchor
lines and fishing nets, incidentals that make evidence
for our bemusement that such a beast could go unnoticed.
It offends us. There's agony in its scanning eye, its tiny
filtering teeth set in that gaping mouth, caught perversely
wide, a universal fellatio, opened to make it look more
than shark enough; and even science will realise
that it's undead, its 'ka' and 'ba' fixed and lost
in equal measure, the flow of fluid not even providing
an optical illusion, no 'weighing of the heart' beyond
the heartlessness of curiosity,
eschatology of display.

BLUE-RINGED OCTOPI

To hunt shores at night evokes a word we lack:
as *greater* frustrates *lesser*, both having deadly
bacterial bites: the painless nip that makes paralysis
look inward though wide awake, watching your
tranquillity of demise. This isn't purely fact
collated from texts, but first-hand news: hand
touching the hand that touches the skin and agitates
a calm rockpool near mangroves to rings of bright
blue that mesmerise: liquid eyes of peacock tails.
Dying mixes metaphors, lays you out flat on the sand.
Welded mouth-to-mouth. Twenty-four hours,
a single breath. Not a breath to be had outside
the host's, breathless you give nothing back.
A marriage against convention and Nature.
That's your brother at twelve saying, 'Watch it move!',
flattened swirls across needles and jags of rock,
eight small legs that collect a space to hold
the pulsing head. Inkless inscription warning
small boys it will strike fingers through water
bending with the sun. Blue wedding rings.
And waiting for an electric shock that never
manifests, to pass through body unto body,
my pulling him away to break the contact.
You rarely feel the bite. And too late
if you do, as there's no cure but breath.

And repeated in cold southern waters, where
the *lesser* lurks in bottles and shells, neat beak
that rips a tiny crab apart, vacuuming flesh. The swell
incites rockpools, and tides bring on the scuttle.
To treasure such poisons — tetrodotoxin, maculotoxin —
the child who picks over innocence, loves risk,
loves fear, half-lulled by the ravaging of that great
amnion, the ocean. Or surrounded by mangroves
up north where it's hot and putrid and salty, where
infection sets into the smallest cut — mangroves'
false sense of security, mudflats stretching out as far
as tides can ever go — blue-ringed octopi lying low
in brine tepid with waiting. Hungry but shy.

Waterwheel by the Oceans

The making of rock never stops:
it is a definition of the universe
that might work. The flow of water
over waterwheel is a mineral
deposit, a washing of a wheel
that can no longer turn, solidified
at the meeting-point of oceans,
the in-betweens of rockpools.

Fresh water spills from a petrified
waterwheel making living hair
of algae, an aesthetic declaration
when lighthouse pulses,
sharp corner of land we cling
to. And as watertable falls,
the spring that falls to marsh
dries out, what's left pumped up
to keep the waterwheel offering
pilgrims perpetual libation.
All around, salt thirsty as ocean.

There are far fewer periwinkles
clinging to rocks now I am much
older than my parents were when
they took me inside this postcard
to pillage rockpools. Granite is resilience,
but limestone overtly living: it makes
its call against the aqueduct, and flow
is sustenance, building spokes
from axle to those great circles
we build religions from, spiritual
affirmation in the light of need:

entertainment, another site
to tick off on the tour, to reconcile
anomalies of fresh and salty water,
the imagined calm of depth
in all its manifestations,
its drawing to surface.

The Merry-Go-Round by the Sea
(Geraldton, Western Australia)

in memoriam Randolph Stow

It's beneath the ficus tree, umbrella
against the breadth of the sea,
but the harbour hedges bets anyway,
and foreshore build-up is profligacy.

Facsimile to start with, fixed
paradox to hear closer the rush
of westerlies, the curl of breakers
around the point. Hustle of town.

It's varied for each of us — centrifugal
or centripetal certainty, according
to our different natures. And the giddy
fascination with where explorers

go to be lost to others, overwhelmed
by bones and light and themselves.
And light through branches, glimmering
of the changeable surface is all here.

It's the technology of wrecks: the metal
of canons, astrolabes, and coins of realms.
An antenna charged by the young, like
a raw colonial future. Blind sunset.

Stopped mid-spin, can it hold its charge,
anchored by a plaque? Son of the town
writes centres, pole we spin around.
His story is our story retold?

Some decline the offer. Some
skip stones out over the water,
a murky leaden colour. Others listen
hard to shells that stay silent,

if they've ever spoken. We've never
felt more alone than swinging on the merry-
go-round with strangers to balance
the compass, making the rules.

I saw an osprey on the foreshore
not far away: its standing shape
not glamorous as in flight, not
deadly as grace. White mottled black,

sand in its claws, its land-lurch.
Out at sea, great ships in their lanes,
bristling with lights. I doubt those
on deck looking in at the shores

would see this monument, the writing
on the walls. They might say 'Batavia Coast'.
They might think of mutiny and death.
They might think of eyelight

shining out at them, a trick of sea
and spray and sun, glinting of sand
especially brought in for the occasion,
making new history to write out again.

The Vitiation of Presence

In those glass-fronted rooms, mannequins
caught in the act reach for the tea service
or prepare to strike a single piano key, a one-
fingered sign of learning, where heavy lace
bunches around the neck and air-conditioning
keeps the old world in place, the deadly sun
through acres of brick and steel in check.

Our daughter who now wants to be a museum
curator would shrink and shake at the sight
of mannequins in period costume: in
castles or settler houses, cavemen with clubs
chasing mastodons thawed from ice and still stuck,
uninterested in escape, that second death
that makes ghosts of ghosts and not even mediums
can hear, so many times dead in their rebirths.

Our son is obsessed with all things old and we
take him to museum after museum. He likes best
the small country museums in situ: pump stations,
old hospitals, gaols rehabilitated into a slice
of life we might learn from, though nobody
is sure quite what. As the mannequin dressed
for Sunday lunch spots the embossed cover
of a collection of Wordsworth's poems

we pass by and embroider our personal histories:
what we remember when labels fade and anachronism
becomes fashion again. She is so much smaller
than the average white middle-class Australian
country woman, someone says, her eyes fixed on
a distance that goes deeper than book or table
or dinner service, and her tanned polyethylene
skin is a disruption of verisimilitude they swallow

for the occasion. A smart-arsed son, visiting family
in the country for the holidays and tagging along
on the weekend outing, might add: 'it's simulacrum'
and alienate his father who thinks he's stuck-up anyway
and lazy and avoiding work at harvest when he's most needed.
But who am I to say, listening in to the living
exhibit as we are also, free of our cases, swanning
between artefacts. I look it up: these mannequins

are made by specialists and have interchangeable
body parts. Dolls for all seasons, bringing fear
and comfort in equal measure. We reach out to touch
their hair and strike the glass which is so much closer
than it seems. In old gaols, judges and prisoners
vitiate each other's presences and we stay silent.

Three Poems on Armour

KNIGHT'S ARMOUR AT THE FITZWILLIAM MUSEUM, CAMBRIDGE

From sabaton to visor, greave to rerebrace:
      (*He knows but one direction!*)
His family call him cyborg, but lack imagination;
He's all metal until an enemy punctures

His undercoating. Chain mail is satisfying
      (*It breathes . . . is coldly sweaty,*)
It imprints on skin or aketon a cartography
Of craftsmanship: he goes to his maker

Well unmade, having driven an economy.
      (*Museums maintain downpayments.*)
In an idle moment he marvels over rivets:
The movement of the poleyns: vital as his kneecaps.

As mirrors of his joinery, steel plate makes faith:
      (*God's handiwork given a good workover.*)
Detailed, custom-lined, in *his* own image — moreover,
Performance enhancing, product placement:

Chivalry! He's the complete package.
      (*He's thrown down the gauntlet.*)
He removes his cuisses and faulds,
And enamours us with his tenderness:

Cheerleaders, weekend warriors
        (*Paintballers outside office hours,*)
Paragliders, scrappers, war gamers,
Dealers fighting turf wars. Soldiers.

        (*Impact of mace on plate shatters peace.*)

Metal Horse Sculpture in Northam Town Park

The hundred-year flood-level would test
its grip — pinioned to concrete in a green field,
space of rest and play. A silver canter, zest
of a foal, war-weary soul sealed
in metal, hollow eyes fixed, annealed
like suns in retreat, charging past children
swinging high out of sandpit — above raised
riverbanks and pine trees — on through the town,
fighting arthritic welds, futurist prison

of cogs locked into place, springs
that won't stretch, never retract. It hears
no birds, though white swans and crows ring
its bells. The wire-mesh stomach hungers
for grass, filled instead with leftover wrappers,
drink-cans, dead condoms. It doesn't know
this place, is confused by the atmosphere —
the stilled, algal river . . . dull bisque glow
of harvested hills, roads bloody with heat haloes.

Its speech consists of silent letters,
mouth always open, ears cocked . . . some try, walking
the park alone, bending down, lending an ear . . .
some want the ear to bend their way, stroking

the bright mane and whispering
to someone lost, elusive — best-kept secrets. Time
stretches for singer and listener . . . lamenting
and praying, wanting revenge . . . the grime
of their breath congeals, forms a dull amalgam.

Here, they make horses work.
No exception. Stallions are gelded. Mares
run into the dirt. The aged sent to lurk
in paddocks beside vats and towers
that stink so bad drivers and passengers
wind up their windows when rushing past.
Iron horses — stuff of memorials — never cower
when faced with fireworks, a blast
of spray-paint, comparisons to glories lost.

The hundred-year flood-level would test
its grip — pinioned to concrete in a green field,
space of rest and play. A silver canter, zest
of a foal, war-weary soul sealed
in metal, hollow eyes fixed, annealed
like suns in retreat, accepts its place
of rest — trapped — moving forward —
shadows burn its reflective surface,
whisperers of communal grace.

DÜRER'S RHINOCEROS

Rhinoceros of childhood seen through thick bars
with sandpit and wagtails, zoo savannah or grasslands,
country compacted to a round peg in a square hole,
resigned in flesh if not eyes — vacuums of desire,
armour the leathern shields of the most ancient myth,
army writ into the single body that carries all
before it. And this Indian specimen, courtier
of language and war, limbs of what *we* imagine
as Sanskrit, resilient exotica, impenetrable with fear.
Second-hand, Dürer made this beast his own
for centuries, never witnessing its drowning
in wild seas, shipped from pillar to post, its second
skin armour on armour, body sculpted, riveted
with bones and cartilage, scales and ivory,
immutable overkill, moulded for comfort
and flexibility, sheer engineering that makes
a gift from king to king, general to general, give
and take of manufacture and manoeuvrability,
statement of homegrown technology you'll think
twice about before taking on. Even dismantling
and back-engineering you'll pull up short — it bears
no imitations. The weight of creature and armour
drives the horn deep into any Achilles' heel, affirmation
of vengeful gods: metal breastplates and cuisses,
backplates and faulds without chivalry you recognise,

like that unfamiliar vestigial horn — clitoral,
to be stroked in violence? — forced to perform
for the royal crowd, artist's impression. You saw
those eyes as a child, behind thick bars, with sandpit
and wagtails, a zooscape shouting 'there are only
a couple of thousand Indian rhinos left, whereas
in Dürer's time there were at least half a million'.
Cause and effect. It would be over sixty years
after the 1515 capturing in ink before another such
sailed to Europe. No longer the prototype,
despite the novelty. Dürer's truth: guardian of spices,
myth incarnate, embodiment of wars Europe was
preparing for. Anatomically suspect.

Two Poems for Peter Porter

Vixerunt

after viewing Vincenzo Foppa's
The Young Cicero Reading (c. 1464)

And yet, to have lived so much already,
the gentle weariness of an angel
who has seen lengthy warring
between good and evil,

but can't wrinkle, can't take
the rouge from his cheeks, though
reading over his experience,
tightens eyes and concentrates

to be free of his condition,
and yet relish it. Optimism
is the default position, like sowing
the wheat crop into dust

and hoping rains will come,
against predictions. You make
your own luck, and luck so made
is logic. Living is knowing.

And now, young Cicero, creating
your precedents, halo of foliage,
poise stark as any window,
tunic soft against architecture,

the case is outlined: who
threatens the state, the heart
of the republic, will be
silent. The good of the people

is the good of the state,
is the state of well-being.
The evidence stacks up.
Pragmatically, in the end,

you'll ask for the cut to be clean
and swift. Here, in the provinces,
we are easily distracted by the promise
of outdoor living — what quality

of air, what perfumes — your hair
helmeted, still as anticipation.
We listen for birds: now thornbills,
now butcherbirds;

but nothing distracts you,
young Cicero, from your reading:
serene as a room, the sky
dark and light at once,

this bower, this cave, where
criminals are disposed of quicker
than words, the silence
of your learning;

so, master of Rome in waiting
who is not of Roman origin,
whose words will heal and kill,
who cannot shelter beyond

senatus consultum ultimum.

THE AMBASSADORS

In cold weather we are as large
as our clothes make us, warding
off failure with diplomatic immunity,
exploring limits of the plenipotent.

We describe for our hosts the place
we come from: it's large and many
weathers threaten its coastlines. Inland
is an entirety inside an entirety,

an infinitum. An island, yet it is endless.
Yes, there is a great heat that underlies
all extremes. Yes, we retain red dust
under our fingernails years after

arriving in the Great City. Our
tastes are not lavish — we will acquire
books and tickets to the theatre,
and sack galleries for their spiritual

worth, but keep social standing
out of discussions. We *will* visit Saint Paul's
and wonder over Donne's sermons,
but no hint of Apostolic Nuncios

will haunt our office. We will offer
up raw materials, generations
of the well-fed. We will admire
the Old Country's astrologers

gazing up through smog,
bringing heaven uncomfortably
close to earth. Back home, our
skies are *so* wide and *so* shining . . .

we remind our hosts at moments
of triumph — 'Water Music'
on the Royal Barge, the Sex Pistols'
performance of 'God Save the Queen' —

our skies are *so* wide and *so* shining.
The embassy ends before it's begun
and yet is never complete — the skull
we bring with us shines through canvas,

our skin, and as we ascend the stairway
to hand in our resignation, the skull
comes into focus — *so* wide, *so* shining,
so willing to trade across harrowed oceans.

Elegy For

in memoriam Dave McComb

Concurrent, we fill the city.
Without, the air is too full
though we break out, as dull
as cotton wool, as sharp as tacks.

A visceral beauty, lipstick
smudge on a glass, knit
as close as shorelight,
dry rasp of wheat-ears.

Heart devout as our sleeves,
flat-out art to taste
the salt of Prevelly Park, laced
with shells that echo.

That's the lyric warped
around the river, higher
function to pleasure,
serenade the sun that grows

on you. We open your eyes
and hear the swell surge
upwards, an urge
to open nocturnes.

It's reputation. The songs
we spool from partial
info. Penitential
rumours, shadows of vocals.

You can't guard flames
in elegies of those you don't
know, of those you can't
pull up on the screen of memory:

which audience we're part of,
which elegy selects success
on the jukebox: a recess
of scores. Freo Doctor

smooths heat, contracts
lengths of summer.
I hear the Prime Minister
defend the Ku Klux Klan

behaviour of his army:
this 'letting off steam'
to melt the dream,
we dance in propaganda.

This is how I relate to you:
'relate', a dirty word
that's grown, a sword
of grammar and syntax.

I passed a house I lived
in — once — yesterday —
cleared away:
development.

I was arrested by a tune
playing over in my head:
obsessive to the point of dead-
head contretemps, living dead

scratching, soon-to-be-dead
tossed about the Freo lock-up,
rag doll aliens, refrain
like sand, bloodstain

in custody; I tell you I witnessed
death washed down the drain;
we cross the Pont, the Seine
with its life-love, its disdain.

Backdrops to write against.
In the cast of space we scored
again. In the cast of space
we hummed the pace

of boomtown and corporate
take-overs, starlings shot down
over the Nullarbor — heading our way,
away, this the end of our stay

as blessed time passes
with each key, in key, a passenger
liner at the quay; who will listen,
fund our croonings again?

Blue verticals, horizontals.
Those double triple quadruple blocks
to join in mansion, a prayer
of rose gardens and river

views, mausoleums and analogies
of travel — locals out — locals
opening night. Up to Four Squares, wander
North, open out. Friends defer

like hauntings, like fashion:
performance: each of us
in each other's pockets
our sleeves, your hearts.

Staving off inevitables,
we watch from ashen tables,
sing higher than Norfolk pines,
this gifting us, this turning

inside out, an aubade
to sunset, horizon's loud
cicatrice, as soothing as a road
torn wide open:

travel jars the mind
and that's the sign
of the times, the crowd
standing still in flight,

to look out on morning:
good morning, good morning,
and I am reminded
how to know, to listen.

Lyrics or Caveats Written on Indian Pacific Train Travelling from Perth to Adelaide

WATTLE

Every year the bright
tremor of wattle,
yellow light
yellow rattle

of stamens and pollen,
collective memory
blocking-in
understorey.

This profusion
of a short-lived galaxy
provokes effusion
and heresy:

choking drought,
whirl of gases,
clearer's rout,
godless

astronomers;
neither good nor bad
can come of it: it lures
us into sacred

utterances: confess
the yellow light
is not bright
enough, or stress

the yellow light
is too bright,
far too bright
for our limited sight.

EACH JOLT

Each jolt of the train
drills me deeper into the gravel
and sand of Dangin, the rain
of metal on metal,

root of wandoo grips
the breakaway. A parrot
traces telegraph wires
and races the train, its lot

not my lot though I claim
against the grain,
towards an arid zone, grim
imprecation

resonating deeper
than each jolt of the train
that drills me deeper
into the gravel of Dangin.

GIMLETS

Gimlets curl us to their angles:
look no further than a cold gleam,
emanations of square pegs forced
into round holes, liquid-boned
delusion, more petrified calm
than greenstick fracture,
the puzzle's key just at hand.
Muscles flex hollow, wrangle
sinew and hunger:
weak soil projecting strength,
shed posts, fence posts, lengths
of timber for 'make do'
tasks we'll rue
left too late, pushed aside.

'I Get a Kick Out of You'/
'What a Wonderful World'

I think of you listening
to the American Songbook
and it doesn't strike me
as a problem to evoke
nor recall the boobook
owl we hear most nights,
as if we can separate
out its words: courtship
from hunting, call to offspring
or rival approaching.

MALLEE

Claws at twilight. Vibrant
sally into magenta
encircling: hence
the flaying out, spindly rant

from root stock
pugnacity,
a growing rock
of centrifuge, cyclotron,

and the bet is on, that beneath
is more than dust
of red blood cells,
powder of rust

to throw trunks out,
a clasp to hold a fading jewel,
suddenness of night sky
and its spools

of starlight
touchable here
more often
than not.

ON SCHEDULE

Passed through the siding
of Southern Cross.
Approaching Lake Julia.
The salty inland wash.

CAVEAT

There's a caveat on the living trees,
but don't chop up the dead wood:
especially not the trunks stretched
hollow, homes of snakes and echidnas.
When it rains hard they drum a bold
message, and when the wind stirs
through these sacred woodlands
they pipe like great church organs.
That's *your* patois.
Understand. Understand.

NEIGHBOURS

No rain came that year
but egrets still stalked
the dry dam, clicking
flakes of mud aside

with their brittle beaks.
Sell off that bush block,
she said to her husband.
If a family make an offer,

knock the price down.
This place is barren,
no rain will come
with you and me alone

on this crumbling land.
The patience
of waterbirds
won't last forever.

Nullarbor Sunrise

Bluebush does its colour codings.
A wedgetailed eagle — chin up — watches
from its stunted perch. Massive.
Sparse resolution of the arid
fills its territory. Flexing,
it displaces the cold
air of night, reserve
of warm air intensive
under its wings, swatches
of salt bush twitching, twitching.

Dead Steer

Upended beside the rail line.
Bloated, dead skin pushed
to bursting, it's glib
to say death has no decorum.
The living dead dash from the train.
They won't be caught malingering — crushed
in the rush of metal — ad lib
their eventual mustering,
ad infinitum.

UTILITARIAN

Alongside the world's longest stretch
of straight railway line
there are squat,
unused towers — maybe old radio
beacons — I don't know —
occurring at distant
intervals; absolved of verticals
it's no surprise eagles
have set their nests
in these structures, to fetch
their prey from obverse
spreads — always facing
as they pivot round,
the flat, sparsely foliated ground
they'll pierce, sound.

CROSSING THE BORDER (IN REALTIME)

1384 ks from Perth.
Saltbush.
Odd *Acacia papyrocarpa*.
Immolation of borders
under over-blue skies.
Beneath, parallel,
fibre optic cable.
Copper telegraph line
gone in rebirth,
sea-flaw.

COOK

The eucalypts
those railwaymen
from both sides of the border
planted to make an oasis
on the limestone plateau,
enwrapped in saltbush,
are said to have failed:
but the perseverance
of eucalypts, pepper
trees, opportunistic or smart acacias,
the sheer zaniness
of mirages on the horizon
with their plimsoll-line
counter-play.

Maralinga

Hell is hollow, a gesture in a flat surface lipped in, the curve upturned — no same point if you keep going in the same direction; convex lore coated longer than words and longer than belief. A weeping tree in flower, a minuscule tree among the saltbush and deceased. A camel skeleton hunched big-boned against the track. Spirit-killer? It's a weapon they'd test a few times at least. Watson siding as water only here was apertured into lexical theft, before and after, to make the big bang, negate and relegate the gathering tribes — a plan — atomic warfare against a people so old they brought fear to investors in peerage, shock wave propelling the train slightly faster once out of Watson, where the first flock of birds seen since yesterday overfly warning markers, pink and grey galahs their chests shields worn in the x-ray rooms, all nature is conflated in the atom and there's no half-life of logic to ward off the insecurities. Clear sky thunder. The name retains. A given name. A Christian name. Exposure to the energy source of God by any sectarian configuration. Mirage of treed islands run blue, like a leak from the sky, blue blood shining over the expanse. Seriously, that's what you see: a spreading blue across the Axminster texture of the plain, as they would envisage it. Still holding the data, using it not an end in itself, down the track. That line of hills to the north. What do they hold back on the edge of the plain, the hollow bones.

Wirangu Meeting Place/Barton Siding

Barton, first prime minister
is the reference point for this vital
meeting place. Go figure.

ZIGGY'S HUMPY AT BARTON SIDING

They moved him off government land
and he moved back again. In the desert
by the railway siding. Died in red sand.

Sunset Approaches, Behind Us (South Australia, heading towards Port Augusta)

Sunset approaches and desert oak
silhouettes against rabbity scrub.
A trick of reversals, the last rays
lance the irregular crowns. A
lack of light wakes and makes
for sleep, written to reap
the flux of worlds apart,
seeps to wide-eyed marsupial,
heady and alert in the desert oak
as light diminishes
and its rights are revoked.

Baudelaire

Ah, *Le Revenant*, like Tim reading off the song titles
of the big-handed gangler, Jacques Brel, Tracy's hero
and subsumer, he of her complete ode I await
to read: a reading, a hearing, this picture to words:

> *So, my wife, in our years*
> *of familiarity — warped angels —*
> *staining freshly washed sheets,*
> *blue with homecoming, night-bright;*
>
> *beneath the rampant moon*
> *snakes coil tight and shots*
> *fracture: roo shooters*
> *just beyond our room;*
>
> *the morning blackens*
> *skin, white sheen*
> *of night, muzzle-flash,*
>
> *bled lightning I leave*
> *again, and our presence*
> *affronts, mouth-hearted.*

ACKNOWLEDGEMENTS

Agni, Antipodes, Australian Book Review, Australian Literary Review, Crazy Horse, Critical Quarterly, Jacket, Meanjin, Overland, Penumbra Magazine, Poetry London, Poetry Review (UK)*, Poetry Wales, London Review of Books, New Yorker, The Age, The Best Australian Poems 2007* (edited by Peter Rose, Black Inc., 2007)*, The Best Australian Poems 2008* (edited by Peter Rose, Black Inc., 2008)*, International Literary Quarterly, Nation, Times Literary Supplement, The Wolf, Vagabond Holes: David McComb & The Triffids* (edited by Chris Coughran and Niall Lucy, Fremantle Press, 2009). 'Vixerunt' was awarded the 2008 Bruce Dawe Poetry Prize.

John Kinsella wishes to thank the University of Western Australia where he is a Professorial Research Fellow. Special thanks to Don Paterson.